Cover photograph: Coronation decorations,
Elm Road, 1953
Back Cover: Lime Street, 1959

First published in 1992 by: The Bluecoat Press,
Bluecoat Chambers,
Liverpool

Typesetting: Typebase Limited
Design: Michael March and Graham Nuttall
Printed by: GZ Printek, Bilbao

LIVERPOOL
Street Names

A Selection by Thomas Lloyd-Jones

Photographs courtesy of the City Engineer, Liverpool City Council

THE BLUECOAT PRESS

Lime Street 1957

Introduction

There are few subjects which give more pleasure and, at the same time, inform a student of local history than the search for the origins of street names. It is a thrill to discover that the names given to the seven streets which formed the core of the newly-created town of Liverpool in the 13th century have endured into the 20th century.

Many of our street names are topographical while others relate to industries, trade and commerce. Therefore, it is not surprising to find in a great port names relating to shipping. Inevitably, there are allusions to the infamous slave trade and, sometimes, to privateering which, in some cases, was simply legalised piracy.

There are reminders, too, of the shipbuilders and the shipwrights who built not only the slavers and privateeers but, also, ships for the Royal Navy. Other street names remind us of the skills and crafts of the men who serviced the ships such as the ropers, sailmakers and ships chandlers. Regrettably, Liverpool's Sailortown, in which for decades so many of these workers plied their trades, has gone, its site having been taken for the new Law Courts. However, in the heart of the city, we are reminded of the ropemakers by the straightness of such well-known streets as Bold Street, Renshaw Street, Great Charlotte Street and the north end of Lime Street, all of which were once roperies or ropewalks.

The names of naval commanders who distinguished themselves in the wars of the 17th and 18th centuries were given to streets in what is now the city centre. These men were very popular with Liverpudlians of the day, particularly members of the Town Council, many of whom had an interest in the West Indies. Many of our naval heroes thus commemorated were made Freemen of Liverpool and I have quoted from the citations recorded in the Town Books. The names of distinguished soldiers of the period and the battles in which they fought are recalled by many street names, as are those of members of the Royal Families.

Certain street names remind us of coaching times, particularly those bearing the names of distant places to which they led, while the names of neighbouring townships which are now suburbs of the city are borne by roads leading to them. During the rapid expansion of the town during the last century, the names of almost every county, town and city in the United Kingdom, not to mention the mountains, rivers, lakes, estates and stately homes, have been applied to Liverpool streets. Mercifully, the Welsh builders who developed so many areas of the city and gave the new streets Welsh names, spared their English-speaking fellow citizens the more unpronounceable names of the Principality.

At one period, London street names were popular here and many are still in use, as I will explain later. Not all London names were borrowed from the capital, as the alphabetical list demonstrates.

In the 19th century, Liverpool had numerous churches and chapels, many of which gave their names to the street in which they stood or to the street or streets leading to them. Many of these are still in use even though some of the churches were demolished long ago. Although several streets were named after men through whose land they were laid, only two named streets after their wives and one, a Welshman, called a street after his mother.

Some early street names were derived from field names but few have survived. However, it is pleasing to see that this practice has been revived on estates developed in post-war years.

The names of famous passenger liners built on Merseyside and registered in Liverpool, whence they maintained a regular trans-Atlantic service, have been given to streets in Walton and Garston.

All those narrow streets and alleys we called weints or wients, a term peculiar to Liverpool according to Picton, have disappeared in the orgy of demolition we have witnessed since the end of the last War.

The names of long-forgotten sports and entertainment and their participants can be found, as can the names of civic dignatories of the past.

There are thousands of streets in Liverpool but only a selection is listed in this booklet. Following the name in the alphabetical list is the postal district number. It is followed by the original, or former name, when I have been able to discover it. Many of these are of great interest for they recall long forgotten events and institutions in the city's history.

Acknowledgement

Thomas Lloyd-Jones was born in 1904 to Welsh-speaking parents in the Princes Park area of Liverpool. He remained in the city all his life and contributed extensively to its heritage, history and adult education.

Life was never easy. His father was killed in a road accident when Thomas was two and this resulted in him leaving school at thirteen to help his widowed mother. However, his passion for learning led to him joining the Workers' Educational Association when he was eighteen and he gave the movement his unswerving support, becoming Chairman of the Liverpool branch and, also, the West Lancashire and Cheshire District. The University of Liverpool recognising his achievements, awarded an honorary Master of Arts, in 1965. After a long illness, he died in 1990.

Thomas Lloyd-Jones made an invaluable contribution to local history. His publications included 'Liverpool Old and New' (1975), 'Liverpool and Wirral' (1978) and Walks in the City Centre (1974) and 'Liverpool Street Names' (first published in 1981).

ABERCROMBY SQUARE *7*

Commemorates General Sir Ralph Abercromby (1734-1801), Commander of the British Army in Egypt who was killed in the Battle of Alexandria in 1801.

ACKERS HALL AVENUE *14*

Ackers Hall was the dower house of Lady Molyneux, the widow of Sir Patrick Molyneux who died in 1568. Afterwards, she married William Moore of Bankhall.

ADDISON STREET *3*

Formerly Sickman's Lane or Deadman's Lane. Named after Joseph Addison (1672-1719) poet, essayist and statesman. The former name was given to the country lane where, in times of plague, sufferers were isolated in cabins. If they died, the poor were buried in the vicinity.

AIGBURTH HALL ROAD and AIGBURTH HALL AVENUE *19*

The original Aigburth Hall was a medieval building which came into the possession of the Tarleton family of Fazakerley through marriage. It was demolished and a modern building bearing the same name was built on the site. That, too, has been demolished.

ALBERT PARADE *3*

It is a riverside walk adjacent to Albert Dock, which was opened by Prince Albert in 1846.

ALLERTON BEECHES *18*

The name derives from a mansion built by Sir Henry Tate, to the design of Norman Shaw, called Allerton Beeches.

ALMA ROAD *7*

Commemorates the Battle of Alma, in the Crimean War, when the Russians were totally defeated in 1854.

ANFIELD ROAD *4*

Derived from Hangfield, the original name of Breckfield Road North.

ARCHERFIELD ROAD *18*

The name was inspired by the so-called Archer's Stone in nearby Booker Avenue.

ARGYLE STREET *1*

Called after John, Duke of Argyll, celebrated by Scott in 'The Heart of Mid-Lothian'.

ASHFIELD *15*

The house which gave the road this name was built by James Clemens, Mayor of Liverpool in 1775 when the seamen's riots took place and the Town Hall was attacked with cannon brought from their ships.

ASHTON STREET 13 and ASHTON SQUARE *25*

They commemorate Nicholas Ashton, owner of the Dungeon Salt Works, Hale, and a ship-owner.

ATHOL STREET *5*

Named after the Duke of Athol, on whom an Honourary Freedom was conferred by the Town Council in 1737.

BALTIMORE STREET *1*

One of the streets laid out by Mr. Hunter, who was engaged in the Virginia tobacco trade and lived in Mount Pleasant.

BANASTRE STREET *3*

Named in compliment to General Sir Banastre Tarleton, MP. Son of John Tarleton, he was born in a house on the corner of Fenwick Street and Water Street. He fought in the American Civil War.

Anfield Road 1905

Aigburth Hall Avenue 1950

BANKHALL STREET *20* — Bankhall was the second home of the Moore family. Its site was about the junction of Juniper Street and Bankhall Lane but about twenty feet above the present ground level. It was demolished in 1770.

BARKHILL ROAD *17* — Named after a mansion called 'Barkhill' on Mossley Hill, first occupied by Thomas Adison who was succeeded by James Howell, a cotton broker. In 1845, Howell's daughter named a ship 'Barkhill' from the Baffin Street yard of Thomas Royden.

BASNETT STREET *1* — Laid out between 1770 and 1780 by the Basnett family of which Christopher was the founder. He was the first minister of Key Street Chapel (licensed in 1707), the meeting place of the Protestant Dissenters.

BATH STREET *3* — The name derives from the sea-water baths erected about 1765. They were demolished in 1817 to make way for Princes Dock.

BEACONSFIELD ROAD *25* — Derives from Beaconsfield House, a mansion built by Ambrose Lee, a solicitor and property owner, who laid out the road. He is thought to have named it in allusion to the beacon on Woolton Hill.

BEAUFORT STREET *8* — Named after the Duke of Beaufort, formerly the Marquis of Worcester, who was the guardian of Charles William, 8th Viscount Molyneux and 1st Earl of Sefton, who was orphaned when eight years of age.

BEAUCLAIR DRIVE *15* — Named after the Duke of St Alban's family, the Beauclerks, who inherited the Speke Estate of the Norris's.

BEECHWOOD ROAD *19* — The name derives from the mansion called Beechwood House, one of a group of Grade Two listed buildings.

BELOE STREET *8* — Named in compliment to Charles Henry Beloe, a civil engineer, who sat as a Liberal for Abercromby Ward on Liverpool City Council from 1892 to 1902.

BENSON STREET *1* — Called after John Benson, the refractory juryman referred to in one of the Letters of Junius addressed to Lord Mansfield, the Lord Chief Justice of the King's Bench.

BENTLEY ROAD *8* — It was named after a thatched cottage in Lodge Lane which was William Roscoe's last home and where he died in 1831.

BERRY STREET *1* — *Originally Colquitt Street.* Henry Berry, Liverpool's second dock engineer, lived in a house on the north-east corner of Duke Street.

BEVINGTON BUSH *3* — It was the name of a thickly wooded valley between Bevington Hill and Everton Hill. An inn on Bevington Hill was called 'The Bush'.

BIRCHFIELD STREET *3* — It was laid out through a field called Birchfield on which three houses were built, one of them owned by William Roscoe, who also owned the field.

BIXTETH STREET *3* Alderman Thomas Bixteth, Mayor of Liverpool in 1701, was complimented by the Corporation for having paved the street in front of his house with his own hands.

BLACKBURNE PLACE *8* John Blackburne, Mayor of Liverpool in 1760, lived in Blackburne House between 1785 and 1790.

BLACK HORSE LANE *13* *Formerly Black Moss Lane.* The former name referred to one of the bogs, or mosses, by which Liverpool was surrounded for centuries. The present name derives from the original inn of that name at the Prescot Road corner of the lane.

BLACKROD AVENUE *24* The name of an estate near Bolton called Blackrod was granted to Hugh le Norris of Speke by John, Count of Mortain in the 12th century.

BLACKWOOD AVENUE *25* It takes its name from the Black Wood, which appears on an enclosure map of 1813, when it was owned by Bamber Gascoyne of Childwall Hall.

BLAKE STREET *3* Named after Admiral Robert Blake (1599-1657), who became commander of Parliamentary forces during the Civil War but, in 1649, was appointed General-at-Sea and won several victories against Prince Rupert, the Dutch and the Spaniards.

BOLD STREET *1* Named after Jonas Bold, who leased land from the Corporation on which St Luke's Church and a ropery owned by James and Jonathon Brookes were built.

BOLTON STREET *3* Perpetuates the memory of John Bolton who, in 1803, raised and equipped 800 men at his own expense. They became known as Bolton's Invincibles. On December 20th, 1805, Bolton fought and won the last duel to take place in the town.

BOOKER AVENUE *18* Josias Booker was a West India merchant who lived in Poplar Grove, Allerton. He was one of the founders of St Anne's Church, Aigburth.

BOTANIC ROAD *7* It was here that the second Botanic Gardens were established.

BOUNDARY STREET *5* It marks the ancient boundary between Liverpool and Kirkdale.

BOWRING PARK AVENUE *16* Sir William Benjamin Bowring gave to the city Roby Hall and Park which was renamed Bowring Park.

BRECK ROAD *4* Breck is an Old English word meaning uncultivated land.

BRECKFIELD ROAD NORTH *5* *Formerly Hangfield Lane.* Hangfield or hongfield means an ancient division of land.

BRIDGEWATER STREET *1* Commemorates the completion and opening of the Bridgewater Canal in 1773.

BRIDPORT STREET *3* Named after Admiral Lord Bridport (1726-1814), a brother of Lord Hood who was second in command on the 'Glorious First of June', 1794, when the French were defeated in a battle fought 400 miles west of Ushant.

Bold Street 1959

BRODIE AVENUE *18 & 19*

John Alexander Brodie, Liverpool's City Engineer (1898-1925). In 1891, he invented and patented football nets and, in 1901, he patented the idea of prefabricating houses from reinforced concrete slabs. He also introduced the idea of using central reservations for tramcars. The first reserved track, Edge Lane to Broad Green, was completed in 1914.

BRONTE STREET *3*

Named after an estate in Everton owned by a Mr Woodhouse who had vineyards in Sicily from which he produced a Marsala wine supplied to the Royal Navy and which Nelson named 'Bronte' after the title conferred on him by the King of Sicily.

BROOKS ALLEY *1*

Joseph Brook, a merchant and a ropemaker, lived in a house in Hanover Street which had an ornamental garden through which the alley was laid.

BROOKLANDS ROAD *13*

Named after the Venerable Archdeacon Brooks (1775-1855), Rector of Liverpool, who owned land in the vicinity.

BROUGHAM TERRACE *6*

Henry Peter, 1st Baron Brougham and Vaux, was a lawyer, Whig politician and Lord Chancellor of England. He was a friend of the Rev. William Shepherd, minister of Gateacre Unitarian Chapel, and it was Brougham who composed Shepherd's memorial tablet in that chapel.

BROWNLOW HILL & STREET *3*

One of the meanings of the word 'low' is hill and so Brownlow Hill means simply 'brown hill'.

BRUNSWICK ROAD *6*

Formerly Folly Lane. It is said that while a painter engaged in repainting street signs was temporarily absent, a lady sympathetic to Caroline, the ill-used consort of George IV, boldly chalked 'Brunswick Place' on the original sign. The painter on returning and seeing the alteration, assumed it had been made by someone in authority and so he copied it. Later Brunswick Place became Brunswick Road. Islington was originally called Folly Lane but it was extended to include Brunswick Road. The Folly was a tall tower built by a man named Gibson on the site now occupied by Wellington Column. At the foot of the tower were pleasure gardens.

BUTTON STREET *2*

John Button was granted a lease on the land through which the street was cut in 1722. He recorded his vote in 1784, having lived through the reigns of six monarchs of England.

BYROM STREET *3*

Formerly Towns End Lane or Dog Kennel Lane. It was named after George Byrom, a pavior and builder, who had a yard nearby. The former names derived from Towns End, the name for the end of Dale Street and from the neighbouring kennels of the Corporation supported pack of hounds.

CALDERSTONES ROAD and AVENUE *17*

The name derives from the Calderstones, the name given to the park created by Liverpool Corporation from the Calderstone Estate purchased in 1902.

Byrom Street 1904

CAMDEN STREET *3*

Sir Charles Pratt, 1st Earl of Camden (1713-1794) was called to the Bar in 1738. He was Lord Chancellor (1766-1770), President of the Council (1782-1794) and was created Earl of Camden in 1786.

CAMPBELL STREET *1*

Formerly Pot House Lane. George Campbell, a West India merchant and sugar boiler, was Mayor of Liverpool in 1763. The name Pot House Lane derived from a pottery.

CANNING PLACE *1*

By a resolution of the Council in May, 1832, 'it was named out of respect to the memory of the late Right Honourable George Canning to whose exertions the Council are so mainly indebted in the assistance afforded them in carrying into effect the plan for erecting a new Custom House and other Revenue Buildings on the abovementioned site.'

CARLTON STREET *3*

Carlton was the name of a leading member of the board of the City of Dublin Packet Company whose premises were nearby.

CARNATIC ROAD *18*

The first Carnatic Hall was built by Baker and Dawson, owners of the privateer 'Mentor', out of part of the proceeds of the sale resulting from the capture of the French East-Indiaman 'Carnatic' in 1799.

CARPENTERS ROW *1*

Commemorates the shipwrights of the neighbouring shipyards.

CARYL STREET *8*

The Molyneux family owned most of Toxteth Park and it was after Caryl, 3rd Viscount Molyneux that this street and Lord Street were named.

CARVER STREET *3*

Mr Carver, Steward to the Earl of Derby had a house there.

CASES STREET *1*

Named after Thomas Case, a brother-in-law of Sarah Clayton.

CASTLE HILL *2*

It took its name from the hill which ran down from Castle Street to the river. Daniel Defoe was entertained in the house of Sam Done on Castle Hill in 1705. It is now only 13 yards long.

CATHERINE STREET *8*

Called after his mother by William Jones (1788-1876), who built houses in the city's Bloomsbury area. He built his own house, 35 Catherine Street, where he lived until his death.

CAVENDISH GARDENS *8*

It is on the fringe of Princes Park, which was laid out by Joseph Paxton, then head gardener to the Duke of Devonshire at Chatsworth. The name perpetuates the association of the Cavendish's with this enterprise.

CAZNEAU STREET *3*

Joseph Cazneau, a merchant, built the first house in the street in 1796.

CHADWICK STREET *3*

Called after the proprietor of a limekiln in the neighbourhood.

CHAPEL STREET *3*

It led to the ancient chapel of St Mary-del-Quay on the water's edge. Chapel Street was one of the original seven streets.

CHATHAM STREET *7*

Called after William Pitt (1708-1778), 1st Earl of Chatham, the 'Great Commoner' and one of Britain's greatest statesmen.

Caryl Street 1906

Church Street 1955

CHILDWALL ABBEY ROAD *16* There never was an abbey in Childwall. The name derives from that of a hotel called Childwall Abbey.

CHILDWALL PRIORY ROAD *16* A farm called Childwall Priory gave its name to the road.

CHRISTIAN STREET *3* A potter named Philip Christian built a house on the corner of the street with material salvaged from the demolition of Gibson's Folly.

CHURCH STREET *1* So called from St Peter's Church, Liverpool's first Corporation Church and the first church to be built in England since the Reformation. It was built (1700-1704), on the site now occupied by the Burton Group, to the design of mason-architect John Moffat, a Lowland Scot. From 1880 to 1922, when it was demolished, it was the pro-cathedral.

CLARENCE STREET *3* Named after the Duke of Clarence, later William IV. He visited Liverpool in 1790 when Clarence Street was laid. The Duke was very popular in Liverpool because he spoke in the House of Lords in favour of the slave trade. In 1799, in recognition of his services, the Freedom of the Borough was conferred on him.

CLAYTON SQUARE *1* Sarah Clayton, who laid out the square and neighbouring streets between 1745 and 1750, was the daughter of William Clayton, MP.

CLEVELAND SQUARE *1* The name commemorates John Cleveland, Mayor in 1703 and Member of Parliament for the Borough (1710-1713).

CLEVELY ROAD *18* The name derives from the mansion called Clevely built by Joseph Leather, a cotton merchant, to the design of Sir Gilbert Scott. It was demolished in 1965.

CLINT ROAD *7* Named after Councillor Francis Anderson Clint, who was a former Chairman of the Watch Committee.

COAL STREET *1* There was once a market for Prescot coal on the corner of Pudsey Street and a weighing machine in connection with it was established in Coal Street.

COCKSPUR STREET *3* The name is a reminder that there was once a cockpit in the street. On its site was built a Dissenter's chapel.

COLLEGE STREETS NORTH, SOUTH & EAST *6* They are all streets adjacent to the Liverpool Collegiate Street.

COLQUITT STREET *1* John Colquitt was Collector of Customs and lived in Hanover Street. His land extended to the present Berry Street.

COMBERMERE STREET *8* Named after Lieutenant-General (later Field Marshal) Stapledon Cotton, 1st Viscount Combermere, upon whom the Council conferred the Freedom of the Borough in 1821.

COMMUTATION ROW *1* So named about the time the Commutation Act was passed to prevent the evasion of window tax by making windows unusually large.

CONCERT STREET *1*

In 1840 a concert hall was built on the corner of the street to replace another destroyed by fire. It is now a bookshop.

COOPER AVENUE NORTH *18*
& COOPER AVENUE SOUTH *19*

Named after Alderman Joseph Cooper, an ironmonger, of Oak House, Aigburth Hall Avenue.

COPPERAS HILL *3*

It got its name from a Copperas Works on the hill which became the subject of controversy because of the foul smells it emitted. It was owned by Richard Hughes, Mayor in 1756, who was prosecuted by the Council and ordered to move the works elsewhere.

CORNWALLIS STREET *1*

Named after Charles, 1st Marquis Cornwallis (1738-1805), Governor General of India (1786-1793) and Governor of Ireland. He negotiated the Peace of Amiens in 1802 and was appointed Governor of India in 1804.

COURT HEY ROAD *16*

The name derives from a mansion called Court Hey, once the home of a branch of the Gladstone family.

CRESSWELL STREET *6*

Mr Justice Cresswell represented Liverpool in Parliament from 1837 to 1842.

CROMPTONS LANE *18*

It takes its name from Dr Peter Crompton who owned Eton Lodge (now Bishop Eton).

CROPPER STREET *1*

Named after James Cropper, a Quaker and philanthropist. He bought the Dingle Bank Estate on which he built three houses for occupation by himself and his two sons. He was a merchant and a ship owner but his ships only carried dummy guns. He was a staunch supporter of the campaign to abolish slavery.

CROSSHALL STREET *1*

Crosse Hall was the Liverpool home of the Crosse family. It stood on the site now occupied by the Municipal Buildings.

CROXTETH ROAD *8*

A reminder that the land on which Princes Park and Sefton Park were laid out was bought from the Earl of Sefton, whose home was Croxteth Hall.

CUMBERLAND STREET *1*

During the 1745 Scottish rebellion, Augustus, Duke of Cumberland, the 'Butcher of Culloden', was supported by a Liverpool regiment which did duty in the defence of Carlisle.

CUNLIFFE STREET *2*

Named after Foster Cunliffe, an enterprising and successful merchant and slave trader who was Mayor in 1716, 1729 and 1735. Inscribed on his monument in St Peter's Church were the words: 'a merchant whose sagacity, honesty and diligence procured wealth and credit to himself and his country; a magistrate who administered justice with discernment, candour and impartiality, a Christian devout and exemplary.'

Clayton Square 1923

CUSTOMHOUSE LANE *1* — This narrow lane led to Liverpool's third Custom House on the quayside of the Old Dock.

DALE STREET *2* — So called because it led to the dale through which flowed the stream from Moss Lake to the Pool of Liverpool. It was one of the original seven streets.

DAMWOOD ROAD *24* — Named after one of the woods on the Speke Estate which for centuries provided the oak from which so many of the Royal Navy's ships were built in Liverpool shipyards.

DAWSON STREET *1* — Named after Pudsey Dawson, Mayor in 1799. He lived in 35 Rodney Street and was especially concerned with the welfare of the blind.

DAULBY STREET *3* — Daniel Daulby of Rydal Mount, Westmoreland, owned the land through which the street was cut. He married Margaret, William Roscoe's only sister, and they took up residence in the street they named Daulby street.

DEANE STREET *1* — So called after Richard Deane who lived in Ranelagh Street but owned a ropery on the site on which the street was laid. It has shortened considerably in recent years.

DENISON STREET *3* — William Denison was the part-owner of the privateer 'Enterprise' and he shared in the £7000 profit from the first three voyages.

DEVONSHIRE ROAD *8* — The name serves as a reminder of the association of the Duke of Devonshire with the creation of Princes Park (see Cavendish Gardens).

DEYSBROOK LANE *12* — The Deys Brook was a very ancient stream running through West Derby.

DERBY SQUARE *2* — Named after Lord Derby who obtained a small grant to enable a small square to be formed for a market on the site of Liverpool Castle.

DINGLE VALE *8* — Derives from the dingle or valley through which a stream ran from High Park, along what is now Park Road to the Mersey. William Roscoe wrote a poem about it when it eventually dried up.

DORANS LANE *2* — Felix Doran was an Irish merchant who lived in Lord Street. He was part-owner of the slave ship 'Bloom' and he shared in the profit of £28123 from the sale of 307 slaves on one voyage alone.

DOVECOTE AVENUE and DOVECOTE PLACE *14* — Dovecote was a mansion built in 1829 by John Torbock.

DRUIDS CROSS GARDENS and DRUIDS CROSS ROAD *18* — The name Druids Cross was given to a house built by Joseph Hornby, a merchant.

DRURY LANE *2* — *Originally Entwhistle Street.* It was in this street that Thomas Steers built a theatre.

DUBLIN STREET *3* — So called after the City of Dublin Steam Packet whose berth was close by.

Duke Street 1950

DUKE STREET *1*   *Originally 'the road to the quary'.* Named in compliment to the Duke of Cumberland. Its original name referred to the quarry which became St James' Cemetery and is now called Cathedral Gardens.

DUNBABIN ROAD *15*   Named after John Dunbabin, who was a local farmer.

DUNCAN STREET *1*   *Originally Hotham Street.* Named after Admiral Adam, Viscount Duncan (1731-1804), best remembered for his victory over the Dutch Admiral de Winter off Camperdown. He was conferred with the Freedom of the Borough as a token of the Council's respect.

DUNDONALD STREET *17*   Thomas Cochrane, 10th Earl of Dundonald, served with distinction in the South African War.

DUNGEON LANE *24*   It leads to Dungeon Point, Hale, where there was once a salt works owned by the Ashton family.

DURNING ROAD *7*   *Originally Rake Lane.* It was called after William Durning, an owner of a considerable amount of land in the area, who built himself a house in the road.

EARLE ROAD *7*   It was laid through the Spekelands Estate of the Earle family.

EBERLE STREET *2*   Philip Eberle owned two hotels in Dale Street and he acted as caterer for the Town Hall for sixteeen years. When he retired, William Street was renamed Eberle Street in compliment to him.

EDGE LANE *7 & 13*   It is an ancient highway so called for its position along the edge of the township of West Derby, parallel with the dividing line between West Derby and Wavertree.

EDMUND STREET *3*   *Originally Mill House Lane.* It was laid out on land belonging to Sir Cleave Moore. When he married, it was named in honour of his bride, Ann Edmund.

EGERTON STREET *15*   Commemorates Francis Egerton, Duke of Bridgewater (of canal fame).

ELDON STREET *3*   Named after Lord Chancellor John Scott, 1st Earl of Eldon, who held office from 1801 to 1827.

ELLIOT STREET *1*   Commemorates Sir George Augustus Elliot, who defended Gibraltar from June, 1799 to 1783.

ERSKINE STREET *6*   Named after Thomas Erskine, a lawyer, who sat in Parliament as a Whig and, in 1806, was made Lord Chancellor.

EXCHANGE FLAGS *2*   This was the name given to the area adjacent to the Town Hall on which, until commodity exchanges were built, merchants gathered to transact their business.

EXCHANGE STREET EAST *2*   *Formerly Juggler Street and High Street.* The Exchange was the present Town Hall.

Eldon Street 1905

FAIRFIELD STREET *7*

The name derives from Fairfield Hall (nicknamed Tea Caddy Hall) built by Thomas Tarleton.

FALKNER SQUARE *8*

Laid out by Edward Falkner, who intended to name it Wellington Square but it was nicknamed 'Falkner's Folly' because it was too far out of town!

FALKNER STREET *8*

Formerly Crabtree Lane. Named after Edward Falkner who, in 1797, enrolled 1000 men in an hour for the defence of Liverpool when a French invasion was threatened.

FARNWORTH STREET *3*

Named after John Farnworth, Mayor in 1865.

FAZAKERLEY STREET *2*

Originally Rosemary Lane. The Fazakerley's of Walton were owners of land through which the street was laid.

FENWICK STREET *2*

Named after Edward Moore's in-laws. His wife was the daughter of William Fenwick of Meldon Hall, Northumberland. The street was sometimes referred to as Phoenix Street or Phenwych Street.

FINCH LANE *14*

Formerly Mockbeggar Lane. The name derives from Finch House, which was built in 1776 by Richard Gildart, who represented Liverpool in Parliament from 1734 to 1754 and was three times Mayor. Mockbeggar Hall was a name usually applied to a grand, ostentatious house where no hospitality was afforded nor any charity given.

FITZCLARENCE STREET *6*

Formerly Clarence Street. As Liverpool absorbed neighbouring townships, street names were often duplicated. As a result, names, usually in the district taken over, were sometimes changed. In this way, Clarence Street, Everton, became Fitzclarence Street, the name given to the Duke of Clarence's children by Mrs Jordan.

FONTENOY STREET *3*

Although the street was not laid until 1790, its name was intended to commemorate the Battle of Fontenoy (1745). It is the only street in Liverpool commemorating a British defeat.

FOX STREET *2*

Named after Charles Fox (1749-1806), a Whig politician who was Foreign Secretary in the 'Ministry of all Talents'.

FREDERICK STREET *1*

Named after Frederick Louis, Duke of Edinburgh, the father of George III.

GAMBIER TERRACE *1*

Named after James, Admiral Gambier (1756-1833). He distinguished himself on the 'Glorious First of June' (1794) and he was commander of the British fleet at Copenhagen (1807), after which encounter he was elevated to the peerage.

GARDNERS DRIVE *6*

Richard Cardwell Gardner was Mayor in 1862.

GEORGE STREET *3*

Named after Prince George of Denmark (1653-1708), the consort of Queen Anne.

Gambier Terrace 1948

Great Charlotte Street 1955

GIBRALTAR ROW *3* — Commemorates the Siege of Gibraltar (1779-1783).

GILDART STREET *3* — Richard Gildart, Mayor in 1731 and 1736, owned land through which the street was cut. He was one of Liverpool's Members of Parliament (1734-1754).

GILLMOSS LANE *11* — This name is another reminder of the many mosses and bogs which isolated Liverpool for centuries.

GORE STREET *8* — Commemorates John Gore, bookseller and stationer, who was the publisher of Liverpool's first directory and of the newspaper, Gore's Liverpool Advertiser.

GOREE *2* — Goree was a bare basalt rock off Cape Verde where slaves were gathered together for shipment to the plantations.

GOWER STREET *3* — Named after Sir John Gower, Chancellor of the Duchy of Lancaster when the castle site was secured for the town. It is one of only two named streets on the dock estate.

GRAFTON STREET *8* — Called after the Duke of Grafton, Whig Prime Minister (1766-1770).

GRAYSON STREET *1* — Named after Edward Grayson, a shipwright, who was killed in one of the last duels to be fought in Liverpool (1804).

GRASSENDALE PARK *19* — The name derives from the ancient place name of Gresyndale or Grese Londale, meaning long, grassy valley.

GREAT CHARLOTTE STREET *1* — Charlotte was the name of King George III's consort.

GREAT GEORGE SQUARE *1* — A statue of George III was to have been erected in the square and the foundation stone was laid on his golden jubilee. The response to the mayor's appeal for funds to complete the project was tardy and years passed before the sculptor could be paid. Eventually, the statue was raised in London Road at its junction with Pembroke Place, now called Monument Place.

GREAT HOWARD STREET *3 & 5* — It perpetuates the name of the great reformer and philanthropist, John Howard. He took a great interest in the planning of the Borough Gaol, which was built in this street in 1786.

GREAT NEWTON STREET *3* — Named after John Newton, once the master of a ship engaged in the slave trade who became a Church of England clergyman. In cooperation with the poet William Cowper, he wrote the Olney hymns, of which the best known is 'Amazing Grace'.

GREENBANK LANE *17* — In 1787, William Rathbone IV bought Green Bank, a farm in Toxteth, for a summer residence and the lane took its name from the farm.

GREENHILL ROAD *18* — The name derives from a mansion called Greenhill built for Sir Henry Tate to the design of Norman Shaw.

GREENLAND STREET *1* — Liverpool's whaling industry was based nearby.

GREENWOOD ROAD *18* — A name inspired by the so-called Archers' Stone in nearby Booker Avenue.

Grafton Street 1956

Greenhill Road 1952

Hanover Street 1947

GRENVILLE STREET SOUTH *1*   *Originally Leveson Street.* Named after Lord Grenville (1759-1834), Foreign Secretary under Pitt after whose death he succeeded as Prime Minister. It was Grenville who, in 1807, introduced the Bill for the abolition of the slave trade. The name of the street was changed because of its notoriety after the murder there of the wife of a ship's captain, his two children and a maid in 1849.

GREYHOUND FARM ROAD *19*   Named after one of the many farms on the Speke Estate.

HACKINS HEY *2*   Called after a tenant of Sir Edward Moore, John Hacking, through whose croft the narrow street was laid. A hey is land enclosed by hedges.

HALL LANE *7*   *Formerly Mount Vernon.* The name refers to Mount Vernon Hall which became a school and, it is said, was attended by Gladstone for a while.

HANOVER STREET *1*   *Originally King Street.* It was called after the reigning family.

HARDMAN STREET *1*   Named after Mrs Hardman, the widow of John Hardman of Allerton, who owned land through which the street was laid.

HARDY STREET *1*   Named after Thomas Masterman Hardy (1769-1839), Nelson's Flag Captain who was with him at Trafalgar when Nelson was killed by a sniper's bullet.

HARRINGTON STREET *2*   *Originally Castle Hey.* The Harringtons of Aigburth owned the land.

HARTHILL AVENUE *18*   Harthill House was built about 1829. In 1848, it was bought by John Bibby, an iron and copper merchant, whose wife was a daughter of Jesse Hartley, the celebrated Dock Engineer.

HATFIELD STREET *7*   The street was laid out on land belonging to the Marquis of Salisbury, whose ancestral home is Hatfield.

HATTON GARDEN *2*   Called after Hatton, near Warrington, the native village of the Johnson brothers who owned the land.

HAWKE STREET *3*   Named after Admiral Edward Hawke, 1st Baron Hawke (1705-1781). His most spectacular exploit was the destruction of the French fleet at Quiberon Bay, which brought to an end plans for the invasion of England. According to Smollett, he was 'the Father of the English Navy.'

HEATH ROAD *19*   It was laid out on what was once Garston Heath.

HEYWORTH STREET *3*   *Originally Church Street.* James Heyworth owned considerable land in the neighbourhood and built a villa in the street named after him.

HIGH PARK STREET, PARKHILL ROAD and SOUTH HILL ROAD *8*   High Park was the highest point in Toxteth Park and, in the 18th century, because of its salubrity, became a popular summer resort for Liverpool folk. The area was often referred to as 'the Richmond of the Mersey'. Parkhill and South Hill are names relating to High Park.

HIGHFIELD ROAD *13* — The name derives from Highfield House, Old Swan. Built in 1763, it became the home of the Dower Duchess of Athol in 1775. She sold the house and estate to her son, the Duke of Athol.

HILLFOOT ROAD *25* — Presumably so named in allusion to Camp Hill.

HOCKENHALL ALLEY *2* — *Originally Molyneux Weint.* The Hockenhalls were a Cheshire family related to the Moores and Sir Edward Moore refers to the house in Dale Street he bought from his cousin, Henry Hockenhall of Tranmere.

HODSON PLACE *6* — The Hodsons were an Everton family who owned much of the land hereabout.

HOLMFIELD ROAD *19* — The name derives from a mansion called Holmfield, once the residence of Sir Thomas Bland Royden and the birthplace of his distinguished daughter Maud Royden, preacher and social worker.

HOLT LANE *25* — It led to Holt Hall Farm, which belonged to the Brettargh family.

HOLT ROAD *7* — When Durning Road was continued through Mr Durning's land, he named it Holt Road after his son-in-law, George Holt.

HOPE STREET *1* — William Hope, a merchant, built the first house in the street on the corner of Hardman Street. The site is now occupied by the Philharmonic Hotel.

HORROCKS AVENUE *19* — Named to commemorate the 300th anniversary of the observation of the transit of Venus over the disc of the sun by Jeremiah Horrocks, 'the founder of English astronomy' (Newton). Horrocks was born in the Lower Lodge of Toxteth Park, at Otterspool, c.1619.

HOOD STREET *1* — Named after Rear Admiral Samuel, Lord Hood (1724-1816), who was made an Honorary Freeman of Liverpool 'in testimony of the high respect this Corporation has for him on account of the very eminent and signal services rendered by him to this country in the late war'.

HOTHAM STREET *3* — Named after Admiral William Hotham, 1st Baron Hotham (1736-1813), who was in action with Rodney, Howe and Hood.

HUNTER STREET *3* — Named after Rowland Hunter, a retired tradesman and tax collector from Cable Street, who built a house on the corner of Byrom Street.

HURST STREET *1* — Called after Thomas Hurst, a shipwright, who was granted a lease of part of The Strand in 1710.

HUSKISSON STREET *1* — Commemorates William Huskisson, MP who was killed at the official opening of the Liverpool and Manchester Railway in 1830.

Hillfoot Road 1921

JAMES STREET *1*

Originally Saint James Street. A shipwright named Roger James lived in a house on Moor Street and it is thought by some historians that it was from him that the street derived its name. However, there is no evidence to support this (James died in 1694). After St James Church, Toxteth was built in 1774, the south end of Park Lane was called St James Street and the original St James Street became James Street.

JERICHO LANE and JERICHO FARM CLOSE *17*

Their name derives from Jericho Farm, one of those created by the Puritans who settled in Toxteth Park in the 17th century.

JOHNSON STREET *3*

The Johnson brothers, bricklayers and builders, owned the land through which Hatton Gardens and Johnson Street were laid.

JUBILEE DRIVE *7*

It was laid out during the Jubilee of George III.

JUDGES DRIVE *6*

It leads to the Judges Lodging in Newsham Park.

KENT STREET *1*

Named after Richard Kent, a merchant and ship-owner, who, in 1768, built himself a handsome house on the corner of Kent Street and Duke Street.

KILSHAW STREET *6*

Laid out by Councillor Kilshaw about 1845.

KING EDWARD STREET *3*

It dates from 1903 and was named in compliment to Edward VII.

KINGSWAY *2*

The name given to the second Mersey tunnel by Elizabeth II when she declared it open on June 24th, 1971.

KNIGHT STREET *1*

Laid out by brothers John and James Knight about 1785.

LANCE LANE *15*

Named after Thomas Lance (1769-1829), an insurance broker and merchant, who was a member of the Wavertree Local Board. Portraits of him, his wife and three children are in Sudley Art Gallery.

LARKHILL LANE *13*

The name derives from a mansion called Larkhill built, in 1760, by Jonathon Blundell of the Ince family of that name. It had a cockpit.

LATHBURY LANE *17*

John Lathbury was the Earl of Sefton's agent and he lived in Toxteth Farm to where the lane led.

LAWRENCE ROAD *15*

It perpetuates the memory of Charles Lawrence, a West India merchant, who was Mayor in 1823 and Chairman of the Liverpool and Manchester Railway at its inaugration.

LEATHER LANE *2*

The name derives from the Leather Hall, a market for leather, which stood there until 1833, when it was moved to Gill Street.

LEE HALL PARK *25*

Lee Hall was built in 1773 for the Okill family.

LEECE STREET *1*

William Leece, a merchant after whom the street is named, lived in Water Street.

LEEDS STREET *3*

Originally Maiden's Green. It was the terminus of the Leeds and Liverpool Canal.

Johnson Street 1935

Low Hill 1955

LEIGH STREET *1*   Elizabeth Leigh was the maiden name of Sarah Clayton's mother.

LIME STREET *1*   *Originally Limekiln Lane.* Where the railway station now stands, there were limekilns in the 18th century. They were dismantled after complaints by the doctors of the Infirmary across the street about the injurious effect of the fumes emitted on their patients.

LISTER DRIVE *13*   It was originated by Thomas Lister, a retired cotton broker, who became Chairman of the West Derby Local Board.

LIVINGSTON DRIVE NORTH and SOUTH *17*   In order to get a good approach to Sefton Park, the Corporation bought twelve acres of land from Joseph Livingston for £12000.

LODGE LANE *8*   It led to the Higher Lodge of Toxteth Park.

LORD STREET *2*   *Originally Molyneux Lane or Lord Molyneux Street.* Molyneux had a house on the north side of Lord Street. After it was demolished, a commercial building called Commerce Court was built on the site and it bore the Molyneux arms carved in stone. The building was destroyed during the last war and the carved arms were lost.

LORD NELSON STREET *3*   Named after Admiral Horatio Nelson (1758-1805), England's greatest naval hero. He was a great favourite with Liverpudlians because, in addition to his professional success, he supported the slave trade. In 1798, he was conferred with the Freedom of the Borough. In acknowledging the honour, he wrote from the 'Victory': 'I was taught to appreciate the value of our West India possessions, nor shall their interests be infringed while I have an arm to fight in their defence.'

LOW HILL *6*   Low means hill as in Brownlow and Spellow.

LUGARD ROAD *17*   Lord Lugard was Nigeria's famous Governor and Commander-in-Chief.

LYDIA ANNE STREET *1*   Called after the wife of George Perry, manager of the Phoenix Foundry to which the street led.

LYNDHURST ROAD *18*   John Singleton Copley, Baron Lyndhurst (1772-1863), was three time Lord Chancellor.

McGREGOR STREET *5*   Alexander McGregor was a merchant who was subsequently manager of the Bank of England branch in Manchester. He owned a house in the street.

MADDOCKS STREET *13*   It is believed to be the only street in the city named after a Roman Catholic priest.

MAJOR STREET *5*   Canon Major Lester, Vicar of Kirkdale, founded the Major Street Ragged School.

MANCHESTER STREET *1* — Before it opened, in 1821, coaches for London, Warrington and Manchester left Liverpool via London Road but they to proceed along Dale Street and the steep hill called Shaw's Brow (now William Brown Street). The creation of Manchester Street enabled them to reach London Road via a widened St John's Lane, which presented a much easier gradient.

MANESTY'S LANE *1* — Joseph Manesty was a merchant and ship-owner who lived on the corner of the street and whose garden was famous for its lavender.

MANN ISLAND *3* — *Originally Mersey Island.* It was an artificial island between George's Dock and Canning Dock on three sides and the Mersey on the west. It lost its water on the north and east sides with the conversion of George's Dock into the building site for the Pier Head buildings. It gets its name from John Mann, an oil-stone dealer, who died there in 1784.

MARINERS PARADE *1* — It led to the Old Dock and was an approach regularly used by seamen.

MARYBONE *3* — A name given at the request of some Catholic inhabitants of the neighbourhood.

MARYLAND STREET *1* — Named in compliment to his trade by Mr Hunter, a Virginia tobacco merchant, who lived in Mount Pleasant and whose gardens extended to the street.

MASON STREET *7* — Edward Mason, a timber merchant, built a house near the north end of the street about 1800. His gardens and grounds extended the whole length of Paddington as far as Smithdown Lane. He built St Mary's, Edge Lane, at his own expense.

MATHER AVENUE *18 & 19* — Commemorates Arthur Stanley Mather, a solicitor, who was Mayor in 1915-16.

MENLOVE AVENUE *18 & 25* — Called after Alderman Thomas Menlove (1840-1913), a draper and Chairman of the Health Committee.

MERE LANE *5* — Domingo Mere extended from Mere Lane to Beacon Lane, Everton. In winter, it was very popular with skaters and members of the local curling club. It was known locally as St Domingo Pit.

MELWOOD DRIVE *12* — A hybrid name given to the playing field of St Francis Xavier School, made up from the first syllables of the names of the two priests who founded it, Melling and Woodlock.

MILE END *5* — So called because it is exactly one mile from the Exchange, now the Town Hall.

MILL STREET *8* — *Formerly Bedford Street.* The name derives from a windmill, which stood on the spot that is now the junction of Hill Street and Mill Street. It was one of many in the area, which became known as 'Little Holland'.

MONUMENT PLACE *3* — The site of an equestrian statue of George III (see Great George Square).

Menlove Avenue 1932

Monument Place 1897

Moorfields 1955

MOOR STREET *2*

It was laid out by Sir Edward Moore about 1665. Originally, it ran from Castle Street down to the shore.

MOORFIELDS *2*

Originally Moor Croft. It was the site of a portion of the Moore family estate, first mentioned in 1697.

MOSS STREET *6*

Thomas Moss of Whiston, father of John Moss of Otterspool, bought land on the road to Low Hill through which the street was laid.

MOUNT STREET *1*

It led to a pleasure garden called Mount Zion, or St James Mount. It was on this site that the Anglican Cathedral was built.

MOUNT VERNON STREET *7*

It led to Vernon's Hall and it was so named about 1804.

MUIRHEAD AVENUE *13*

Commemorates William Muirhead, Chairman of the Health Committee.

NETHERFIELD ROAD NORTH and SOUTH *5*

The name derives from an ancient field name meaning 'the higher or upper field'.

NEW BIRD STREET *1*

Named after Alderman Joseph Bird. a slave trader, who was Mayor in 1746. A street between James Street and Redcross Street had been named in his honour but it was abolished in the 18th century and New Bird Street was named in replacement.

NEW QUAY *3*

New Quay was a river wall suggested by Sir Edward Moore to arrest erosion.

NEWLANDS STREET *6*

Named after James Newland (1813-1871), Liverpool's first Borough Engineer.

NEWSHAM DRIVE *6*

The name derives from the Newsham House Estate bought by the Corporation in order to create a public park.

NORRIS GREEN ROAD *12*

The name derives from 'Norris Green' a mansion, erected by the West Derby branch of the Norris family. The estate was purchased by the Corporation in 1924 and the mansion was demolished in 1931.

NORTH STREET *3*

Named after Lord North, Tory Prime Minister, 1770 to 1782.

NORTH JOHN STREET *2*

Formerly Saint John Street. So called from lands belonging to the chantry of Saint John in the Church of Our Lady and Saint Nicholas.

NORTH SUDLEY ROAD *17*

The name derives from a mansion called 'Sudley' on Mossley Hill. Built by Nicholas Robinson, a corn merchant and Mayor in 1828, it is now an art gallery housing a collection of paintings and furniture bequeathed to the city by Miss Emma Holt.

OAK HILL PARK *13*

So called from Oak Hill House, built by Richard Wyatt in 1773. When the Ladies' Walk at the north end of Liverpool was doomed, Wyatt acquired the oak trees which lined it and had them transplanted in the grounds of his mansion.

OAKLAND ROAD *19*

It derives from 'Oaklands', the home of Sir Alfred Lewis Jones (1846-1909), ship-owner and philanthropist and founder of the Liverpool School of Tropical Medicine.

Newlands Street 1964

New Quay 1955

North John Street 1948

Paradise Street 1948

OIL STREET *3* There was once an oil crushing works in this street owned by a firm called Earles and Carter.

OLD CHURCHYARD *2* The name refers to the churchyard of Liverpool's parish church, Our Lady and Saint Nicholas.

OLD HALL STREET *3* *Formerly White Acres Street or Peppard Street.* The mansion house and seat of the Moores was originally called More Hall. When they moved to Bank Hall, the family referred to More Hall as the 'Old Hall', and so the street leading to it became known as Old Hall Street.

OLD HAYMARKET *1* A haymarket was held there up to 1841.

OLD POST OFFICE PLACE *1* In 1800, the Post Office was moved from Lord Street to Post Office Place. In 1839, business having increased substantially, it was moved to Revenue Buildings, better remembered as the Custom House, Canning Place.

OLD ROPERY *2* William Bushell, a tenant of Sir Edward Moore, lived in Castle Street and had a long garden which he converted into a ropery. This provoked Moore and there was a long argument between them over the enterprise.

OLDHAM STREET *1* It was named after Captain James Oldham, who built the first house in the street. He was engaged in the Middle Passage, the Africa to West Indies section of the triangular route followed by the slave traders. Oldham died at sea in 1825.

ORFORD STREET *1* Named after Orford Hall, Warrington, the seat of John Blackburne.

ORFORD STREET *15* Called after his sister-in-law, Miss Orford, by Dr Kenyon, who laid out land adjoining his house in High Street, Wavertree. Orford Street was part of the development.

ORMOND STREET *3* James, Duke of Ormond, was a statesman during the reign of Queen Anne when the street was laid out.

OTTERSPOOL DRIVE *17* The name given to the carriageway between the bottom of Mersey Road and Jericho Lane when Otterspool Promenade was completed. An attempt to apply the name to Jericho Lane was frustrated.

PARK LANE *1* *Originally 'the road to the park'.* The park was Toxteth Park.

PARK ROAD & PARK STREET *8* These too derive from Toxteth Park.

PARKFIELD ROAD *17* 'Parkfield' was the former residence of Robert Gladstone, Snr.

PARLIAMENT STREET *8* *Originally Townsend Lane.* So called after the Act of Parliament of 1773 created the new town of Harrington. It was the boundary between Liverpool and Toxteth Park.

PARADISE STREET *1* *Originally Common Shore.* Thomas Steers, the engineer who built the first Liverpool Dock, owned land on Common Shore which he named Paradise Street after the street of that name in Rotherhithe, London, where he once lived.

PARR STREET *1* Commemorates Thomas Parr, the banker, who built the house in Colquitt Street which became the Royal Institution. He boasted that he had the handsomest house, wife and horse in Liverpool.

PETER'S LANE *1* *Originally Peter Street.* The name derives from St Peter's Church in Church Street.

PHYTHIAN STREET *6* So called after the publican who built houses in the street.

PICKOP STREET *3* The name derives from a firm of brewers (Pickop and Miles) who once had a brewery in the street.

PIER HEAD *3* A stone pier, built in the 1760's, known as the North Pier, jutted out into the river from a site opposite St Nicholas's Church.

PILGRIM STREET *1* *Originally Jamieson Street.* Named after a privateer called 'The Pilgrim', which brought into Barbados a prize which, along with her cargo, sold for £190,000.

PITT STREET *1* Named after William Pitt the Elder, 1st Earl of Chatham and Prime Minister, 1756.

PLUMPTON STREET *6* It was laid out by Sam Plumpton, a landowner and a member of the Town Council from 1842-1845.

PORTER STREET *3* Named after Thomas Colley Porter, Mayor in 1827, who won one of the most corrupt elections in Liverpool's history.

PORTLAND STREET *5* Called after Henry Cavendish-Bentinck, 3rd Duke of Portland (1738-1809), twice Prime Minister in 1783 and 1807-09.

POWNALL SQUARE *3* William Pownall, a merchant and Mayor in 1767, died of a chill caught while quelling a riot on Devil's Acre, near Salthouse Dock, during his year in office. The square is named after him.

PRESCOT ROAD *7 & 13* In the 17th and early 18th centuries, Liverpool's coal was brought from Prescot by pack horses and an occasional wagon. In wet weather, the road became impassable for wheeled vehicles and, due to the increased demand created by the town's expanding population and industries, the Council obtained Parliamentary permission to turnpike the road (1726). In 1759, the road from Prescot to Warrington was turnpiked, thus enabling coaches and wagons from Liverpool to join the north/south road connecting with London and the main provincial centres.

PRICE STREET *1* The Prices were Lords of the Manor of Birkenhead and they were connected with the Clevelands who laid out this street.

PRINCE ALFRED ROAD *15* *Originally Cow Lane.* It was renamed when Prince Alfred, Duke of Edinburgh, visited Liverpool in 1866 as the guest of S R Graves, MP, at the Grange, Wavertree.

PRINCE WILLIAM STREET *8* Commemorates King William of Orange.

Pownall Square 1906

PRINCES BOULEVARD and PRINCES ROAD *8*

Opened in 1846 and so called because they led to Princes Park.

PRINCES PARADE *3*

It leads from St Nicholas Place to Princess Dock. It was to have been called Royal Parade.

PRUSSIA STREET *3*

So called after the allegiance between England and Frederick the Great in the mid-18th century. George Stubbs, the painter, lived in a house on the corner of Prussia Street.

PUDSEY STREET *1*

Named after Pudsey Dawson, a merchant and shipowner. Mayor in 1799, he was colonel of a regiment of volunteers raised in 1798.

QUEENSWAY *1*

The first Mersey Road Tunnel opened and named by George V on July 18th, 1934.

QUAKERS ALLEY *2*

A Friends Meeting House was erected in Hackins Hey, in 1706, and attached to it was a burial ground. The Quakers left for Hunter Street about 1796, after when the premises became a school.

QUEEN STREET *3*

It was started during the reign of Queen Anne. It was once the centre of Liverpool's Welsh community.

RAINFORD GARDENS and RAINFORD SQUARE *2*

Peter Rainford, Mayor in 1740, bought a piece of land on the bank of the Pool of Liverpool and he laid it out as a market garden.

RAMSBROOK ROAD and RAMSBROOKE CLOSE *24*

They were named after one of the many streams which threaded their way through the Speke Estate to the Mersey.

RANELAGH DRIVE *19*

It was laid out on what had been Lewis's staff sports ground.

RANELAGH STREET *1* **and RANELAGH PLACE** *3*

The Ranelagh Tea Gardens stood on the site now occupied by the Adelphi Hotel. The name derives from the elite 18th century Ranelagh Gardens in Chelsea, London.

RATHBONE STREET *1*

So called after the Rathbone family who owned the land.

RENSHAW STREET *1*

The brothers John and Edward Renshaw owned a ropery on the site of which the street was laid, hence its straightness.

RICHMOND STREET *1*

Named after Dr Sylvester Richmond, a celebrated physician, philanthropist and Mayor in 1672.

RIGBY STREET *3*

Gilbert Rigby, a merchant, lived on the corner of Old Hall Street when Rigby Street was laid out.

ROCK STREET *13*

Recalls a quarry which provided much of the stone used in the construction of Liverpool's docks and buildings.

RODNEY STREET *1*

Named after Admiral George Brydges, 1st Baron Rodney (1718-1792) after his victory over the French, under Count de Grasse, off St Lucia in the West Indies (1782). He was rewarded with a peerage and a pension of £2000 a year.

ROE STREET *1*

William Roe, a merchant, lived in Queen Square in a house which became the Stork Hotel.

Princes Road 1921

St Anne's Street 1955

ROSCOE STREET *1*   William Roscoe, Liverpool's 'greatest son', was born in the Bowling Green Inn at the top of Mount Pleasant but some confusion has arisen because there was another Bowling Green Inn lower down Mount Pleasant, opposite Roscoe Street, which Roscoe's father owned later.

ROYAL MAIL STREET *3*   *Formerly Warren Street.* The change of name occurred when the new Post Office Building in Copperas Hill was opened in 1977.

RUMFORD STREET *2*   A soup kitchen established to Count Rumford's plan once stood on adjacent land.

RUPERT HILL *6* and **RUPERT LANE** *5*   Prince Rupert, the favourite son of Elizabeth, Queen of Bohemia, and a nephew of Charles I, was a general in the Royalist army during the Civil War. He took Liverpool, in 1644, and made his headquarters in a cottage on Everton Brow.

RUSSELL STREET *3*   Admiral Edward Russell, Earl of Oxford (1653-1727) is remembered as the commander of the combined British and Dutch fleets which utterly defeated the French at the Battle of La Hogue in 1692.

ST ANNE STREET *3*   The name derives from St Anne's Church, built in 1772. In the 18th and early 19th century, it was the most fashionable residential street in Liverpool.

ST DOMINGO ROAD and ST DOMINGO VALE *5*   Named after an estate owned by George Campbell, a West India merchant, who owned a privateer which captured a prize called St Domingo.

ST JAMES STREET *1*   The name derives from St James Church, Toxteth. Thereafter, the upper part of Park Lane was called St James Street.

ST JOHN'S LANE *1*   *Formerly Fall Well Lane.* The name derives from St John's Church, which stood in what is now called St John's Gardens, at the back of St George's Hall. Its former name comes from the Fall Well, in Lime Street, for long the town's principal spurce of water.

ST PAUL'S SQUARE *3*   St Paul's Church was built in 1769 on what was then known as 'the Dogfield'. The square and neighbourhood came to be called 'the Belgravia of Liverpool'.

ST VINCENT STREET *3*   It was named after Admiral John Jervis, 1st Earl St Vincent (1735-1823). He was elevated to the peerage after his great victory over the French fleet off Cape St Vincent, in 1797. He was presented with an address of thanks by the Council.

SANDON STREET *8*   Lord Sandon, afterwards the Earl of Harrowby, was a Member of Parliament for Liverpool from 1835 to 1842.

SANKEY STREET *1*   The name suggests an allusion to the Sankey Canal, of which Henry Berry (who lived in a house on the corner of Duke Street and Berry Street) was the engineer.

Scotland Road 1908

SCHOOL LANE *1* — *Originally Ware Street.* The name School Lane was applied when the grammar school founded by John Crosse took over the premises first built for the Blue Coat Charity School.

SCORE LANE *16* — It is one of the oldest roads in Liverpool's suburbs. Score means 'to pasture'.

SCOTLAND ROAD *3* — One of Liverpool's turnpike roads, it led to Preston via Walton, Burscough and Maghull. Stage coaches from Liverpool followed this route through Lancaster and Kendal to Scotland.

SEEL STREET *1* — Thomas Seel, a merchant and property owner, had a house in Hanover Street with extensive gardens through which the street was laid.

SHAW STREET *6* — It was laid out by John Shaw, a Liverpool Councillor, whose father had inherited through marriage the extensive Everton estate of the Halsall family. It was a prestigious residential street in which the first house was built in 1829.

SHEIL ROAD *6* — Named after Alderman Richard Sheil, a merchant, who in his day was the only Catholic Irishman on the Town Council. The adjacent park is also called after him.

SIR THOMAS STREET *1* — *Originally Sir Thomas's Buildings.* It commemorates Sir Thomas Johnson, Mayor in 1715. He represented Liverpool in ten Parliaments. He died in penury in London, in 1728.

SLATER STREET *1* — Named after Gill Slater, who was the first captain of the Liverpool Volunteers raised, in 1766, when a French invasion was threatened.

SLEEPERS HILL *4* — Parts of the common land in the neighbourhood were called Great and Little Sleeper. They were first enclosed by a shoemaker and called Cobbler's Close.

SMITHDOWN LANE *7* **and SMITHDOWN ROAD** — These two highways are amongst the oldest in Liverpool. They led to Esmedune, a manor mentioned in the Doomsday Book. Smithdown derives from Esmedune and means 'smooth slope'.

SOUTH JOHN STREET *1* — *Formerly Trafford's Weint.* So called after Henry Trafford, Mayor in 1740.

SPARLING STREET *1* — John Sparling, Mayor in 1790, projected Queens Dock, which he proposed to construct at his own expense but then sold to the Corporation for the same purpose.

SPARROW HALL LANE *9* — A black and white cottage in the valley, known anciently as 'the Moss', was called Sparrow Hall.

SPEKE HALL ROAD *25* — It takes its name from Speke Hall, the home of the Norris family.

SPEKELAND ROAD *7* — The name derives from 'Spekelands', a mansion built by Thomas Earle, Mayor in 1787.

SPELLOW LANE *4*

'Spellow' means 'Speech Hill' or mount, usually the centre of an administrative area called a hundred. The site on which Spellow Mill stood may have been the original Spellow, for when the mill burnt down in 1828, it was thought to have been five hundred years old.

SPENCER STREET *6*

Spencer James Steers, a grandson of Thomas Steers, the Dock Engineer, owned land in Everton through which two streets were laid, one of which was Spencer Street.

SPOFFORTH ROAD *7*

So called after Frederick Robert Spofforth, an Australian cricketer of the 1870's nicknamed the 'Demon bowler'.

SPRINGWOOD AVENUE *25*

The name derives from Springwood House, built by William Shand, an owner of plantations in the West Indies, who called it after his Antigua home. The drawing room and library were said to have been copies of rooms in Windsor castle.

STANHOPE STREET *8*

Stanhope was the family name of the Earls of Harrington. The 1st Earl of Sefton married Isabella Stanhope, the daughter of the Earl of Harrington.

STANLEY ROAD *2 & 5*

It was laid out by Lord Derby about 1862.

STANLEY STREET *1*

Originally New Street. It was laid out in 1740 through land bought by the Derby family from the Moores of Bankhall.

STEBLE STREET *8*

Called after Colonel R F Steble, Mayor in 1874/75 who, in 1879, presented to the town the fountain at the top of William Brown Street.

STOCKTON WOOD ROAD *19*

Named after one of the many woods on the Speke Estate.

STOWELL STREET *7*

Named after Rev Hugh Stowell Brown, minister of the Myrtle Street Baptist Church which stood on the corner of Myrtle Street and Hope Street.

STRAND STREET 1 and THE STRAND *2*

Originally the shore between high and low water. In the 1850's, the block of buildings in Strand Street between Redcross Street and Crooked Lane had so many sailmakers that it came to be called 'the Sailmaker's Home'.

SWEETING STREET *2*

Originally Elbow Lane. Named after Alderman Sweeting, Mayor in 1698.

TABLEY STREET *1*

So called by William Pownall, Mayor in 1767, through whose land the street was laid out. He came from Tabley in Cheshire.

TAGGART AVENUE *16*

Alderman Gregory Taggart was an Irishman who, at one time, was a collector for the Royal Liver Friendly Society. He was nominated for election to the Council by the Nationalist Society.

Smithdown Road 1955

William Brown Street 1948

TEMPEST HEY *2* — The Plumbes of Plumbe Hall, Wavertree, who had acquired a good deal of land from the Moores, succeeded by marriage to the estate of Sir George Tempest of Tong Hall, Yorkshire. They took the name Plumbe Tempest, hence Tempest Hey.

TEMPLE COURT, TEMPLE LANE and TEMPLE STREET *2* — The name Temple derives from an office complex built by Sir William Brown, to the design of Sir James Picton, called 'The Temple'.

TEWIT HALL ROAD *24* — Derived from the name of a farm on the Speke Estate. On early maps, it appears as Pewit Hall Farm.

THE VINERIES *25* — It got its name from a house and estate once the residence of Thomas Charles Clarke.

TITHEBARN STREET *1* — *Originally Moor Street.* Lord Molyneux, Lord of the Manor, built his tithe barn in Moor Street, in 1514.

TRAMWAY ROAD *17* — Stables and a carriage shed for the horse trams of the Liverpool Tramway Company were built in this road.

TUNNEL ROAD *7* — Derives from the railway tunnel from Edge Hill to Lime Street.

UNION STREET *3* — Named in honour of the union of England and Scotland in 1717.

ULLET ROAD *8 & 17* — Originally Owlet Road.

UTTING AVENUE *4* **and UTTING AVE EAST** *11* — Sir John Utting, who was Liverpool's first 'club doctor', was Lord Mayor in 1917/18.

VANDRIES STREET *3* — A Dutchman named Vandries once occupied an ancient hostelry which was known by his name.

VAUXHALL ROAD *3 & 5* — *Originally Pinfold Lane.* Vauxhall was the name of a house on the banks of the Leeds and Liverpool Canal past which the road led. The name derives from Vauxhall Gardens in Lambeth, London, in the 18th century.

VICTORIA STREET *1 & 2* — Named after Queen Victoria. It was laid out in the 1860's to provide a new approach to Lime Street Station and St George's Hall.

VIRGINIA STREET *3* — Derives from the Virginia tobacco trade which flourished in Liverpool in the 17th century.

WALTON HALL AVENUE *4 & 11* — The mansion, after which the road was called, was bought by John Atherton, a merchant and slave trader, in 1746. His son and grandson sold it to another slave trader, Thomas Leyland, in 1804.

WARREN STREET *3* — Named after Admiral Sir John Borlase Warren (1753-1822). In 1794, he defeated French squadrons on two occasions and, in 1798, he intercepted and defeated a French fleet on its way to Ireland. For this last victory, the Council conferred on him the Freedom of the Borough.

WATER STREET *2* — *Originally Bank Street or Bonke Street.* It was one of the original seven streets and it was so called because it led to the shore or riverbank.

WATERHOUSE STREET *5* — Named after Nicholas Waterhouse, a merchant, who about 1806, bought a house which William Clarke, the banker, had built there before 1790.

WATERLOO PLACE *1* — So called from 'The Waterloo', a public house which also gave its name to the Waterloo Cup for coursing.

WELLINGTON ROAD *8* — Named after the Duke of Wellington after his famous victory at Waterloo, in 1815.

WHITLEY STREET *3* — Named in compliment to Edward Whitley, MP. He was the leader of the Tory Party on the Council before his election to Parliament and his name was a household word in Liverpool.

WILLIAM BROWN STREET *3* — *Originally Shaw's Brow.* Named in compliment to Sir William Brown, who gave to the town the Museum and Library.

WILLIAMSON STREET *1* — The Williamson family owned a great deal of property in the neighbourhood and they laid out the street in the third quarter of the 18th century.

WINDOW LANE *19* — The name derives from Quindale, which deteriorated to Whindale and thence to the modern Window Lane.

WOSTENHOLME SQUARE *1* — The Wostenholme family owned the land on which it was built. It was the first enclosed garden constructed in Liverpool.

YEW TREE LANE *12* — The name derives from a mansion called Yew Tree House, so named after the ancient yew which grew in its grounds.

YORK STREET *1* — *Originally George Street.* The name was changed when Edward Augustus, brother of George III, was made Duke of York and Albany.

GROUPS OF NAMES WITH A COMMON THEME

There are many groups of streets with a common theme, often topographical. Here is a selection of names:

BOTANICAL *7* — In close proximity to the site of Liverpool's first Botanical gardens, opened in 1802 (many years before Kew Gardens), are ALMOND, CHESTNUT, OLIVE and GROVE STREETS.

CUNARD LINERS *7 & 8* — LUSITANIA, MAURETANIA, IVERNIA and SAXONIA ROADS.

CUNARD LINERS *19* — CAMPANIA, CARONIA and LUCANIA STREETS.

DICKENS *8* — COPPERFIELD, DARNLEY, DICKENS, DOMBEY, DORRIT, MICKAWBER, NICKLEBY, PECKSNIFF, PICKWICK and WELLER STREETS.

ECCLESIASTICAL *6* — ABBEY, CATHEDRAL, CHAPEL, MONASTERY, BISHOP, CANON, VICAR, RECTOR and CURATE STREETS.

Williamson Square 1954

ELIAS *1 & 4* A firm of Welsh builders, Owen and William Owen Elias, laid out several roads in Walton which were given names the initial letters of which spelled the firm's title: OXTON, WINSLOW, ETON, NESTON, ANDREW, NIMROD, DANE, WILBURN, ISMAY, LIND, LOWEL, INDEX, ARNOT, MAKIN, OLNEY, WELDON, EUSTON, NIXON, LISTON, IMRIE, ASTON STREETS and STUART ROAD.

ELIAS *4* William Owen Elias built houses in the City Road area and the streets were given the names which spelled the initial letters of his eldest son, E. Alfred Elias: ESPIN, ASKEW, LINTON, FRODSHAM, RIPON, EMERY and DYSON STREETS.

FLOWERS *5* CROCUS, PANSY, DAISY, WOODBINE and HAREBELL STREETS.

GIRLS' NAMES *4* ELSIE, GERTRUDE, MIRIAM and EDITH STREETS.

HOLY LAND *8* DAVID, ISAAC, JACOB and MOSES STREETS.

RUSSIAN *7* In the absence of the evangelist, Heber Radcliffe of Sun Hall, on a mission to Russia, his family decided to develop land in Stoneycroft in which he had an interest . As a surprise for him on his return, they named the new roads KREMLIN, MOSCOW and RUSSIAN DRIVES.

SALISBURY FAMILY *7 & 15* CECIL, HARDWICK, MONTAGUE, HYDE STREETS and CRAMBOURNE and SALISBURY ROADS

WALTER SCOTT *17* MANNERING, MARMION, WAVERLEY and IVANHOE ROADS.

SHAKESPEARE *19 & 20* ROMEO, JULIET, MACBETH, OTHELLO, PORTIA, FALSTAFF and SHAKESPEARE STREETS.

SOLOMON *7* A quack called Samuel Solomon sold a concoction he called 'Balm of Gilead', from which he made a fortune out of which he built a mansion, in Kensington, called Gilead House. When it was demolished, three streets were laid out on the opposite side of Kensington called GILEAD, SOLOMON and BALM STREETS.

TENNYSON *8* GWENDOLINE, GERAINT, ENID, ELAINE, CLARIBEL, MAUD, MADELAINE, SHALLOT and MERLIN STREETS.

There are many more such groups but they are mostly topographical

LIVERPOOL STREET NAMES BORROWED FROM LONDON

In the 18th century, it became the fashion to borrow London street names for Liverpool streets. In a guide published in 1797, the author W. Moss said; 'the stranger will have discovered a tendency here to ape the London names of places, but which is to be feared of will, on comparison, tend to lessen in his estimation what he might otherwise have considered as neat or commodious'.

The London street names which have survived are: CHEAPSIDE, CORNHILL, COVENT GARDEN, DRURY LANE, FLEET STREET, KENSINGTON, NEWINGTON, PADDINGTON, PALL MALL, WAPPING and WHITECHAPEL.

The London street name Cheapside derives from the 'cheapside' of a street market but there is no evidence to suggest that Liverpool's Cheapside ever had a market nor do its former names Dig Lane, Duck Lane, Barne Hill or St Patrick's Hill suggest as much.

Pall Mall in London gets its name from a game and the Italian words palla (a ball) and maglio (a mallet).

Soho was an old hunting cry and it was applied to the London area, now called Soho Square, where a hunt once met. Although Liverpool Corporation once supported a pack of hounds, there is nothing to suggest that it was associated with the city's Soho Square.

Fleet Street in London took its name from a stream but at the time Liverpool's Fleet Street was named it could bost no stream, only two breweries and a few houses.

Islington 1900